I0796614

AV2

www.av2books.com

Kevin Scarpati
and John Willis

Step 1
Go to **www.av2books.com**

Step 2
Enter this unique code
HVYCU63VD

Step 3
Explore your interactive eBook!

AV2 is optimized for use on any device

Your interactive eBook comes with...

Contents
Browse a live contents page to easily navigate through resources

Audio
Listen to sections of the book read aloud

Videos
Watch informative video clips

Weblinks
Gain additional information for research

Slideshows
View images and captions

Try This!
Complete activities and hands-on experiments

Key Words
Study vocabulary, and complete a matching word activity

Quizzes
Test your knowledge

Share
Share titles within your Learning Management System (LMS) or Library Circulation System

Citation
Create bibliographical references following the Chicago Manual of Style

This title is part of our AV2 digital subscription

1-Year Grades K–5 Subscription
ISBN 978-1-7911-3320-7

Access hundreds of AV2 titles with our digital subscription.
Sign up for a FREE trial at **www.av2books.com/trial**

MINNESOTA VIKINGS CONTENTS

Quarterback Kirk Cousins signed with Minnesota before the 2018 season. Before playing for the Vikings, he played for Washington.

INTRODUCTION

The Minnesota Vikings have never won a **Super Bowl**, but some of the best players in the National Football League (NFL) have played for the team. The Vikings are based in Minneapolis, Minnesota. Their name comes from the people of **Scandinavian** descent who settled the area many years ago. With Cris Carter and Randy Moss leading the way, Minnesota finished with a 15–1 win-loss record in 1998. Since then, they have continued to ride a high-powered offense and tough defense to many wins.

Stadium U.S. Bank Stadium

Division National Football Conference (NFC) North

Head Coach Mike Zimmer

Location Minneapolis, Minnesota

Super Bowl Titles 0

Nicknames The Vikes, The Purple, Purple Pride, The Purple People Eaters, The Purple and Gold

30 Playoff Appearances

4 Super Bowl Appearances

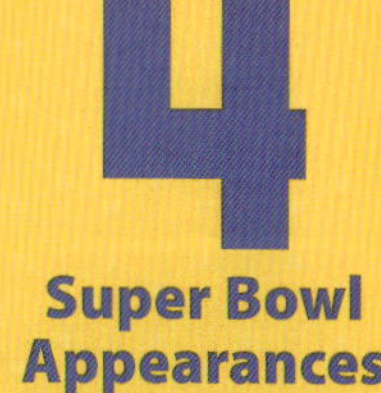

20 Division Championships

FIVE

The Vikings have reached the NFC Championship game five times since 1978.

HISTORY

The Minnesota Vikings were formed in 1960 and played their first NFL season in 1961. They made it to the **playoffs** almost every season during the 1970s. Legendary quarterback Fran Tarkenton led the way.

The 1990s saw the arrival of head coach Dennis Green and a new generation of Vikings legends. During the 1998 season, the Vikings scored 556 points to set a league record at the time. Today's Vikings continue to seek a Super Bowl win.

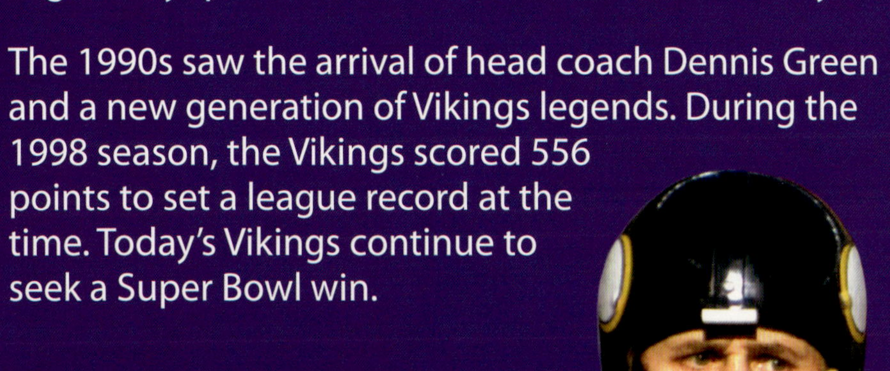

On September 9, 1998, Fran Tarkenton became the first player inducted into the Viking Ring of Honor.

Vikings fans packed U.S. Bank Stadium for its first playoff game on January 14, 2018. The Vikings won 29–24.

THE STADIUM

U.S. Bank Stadium is one of the newest stadiums in the NFL. It opened in 2016. Total construction costs were more than $1 billion. The stadium can hold more than 66,000 fans.

U.S. Bank Stadium has a clear roof that allows sunlight to shine through. Its windows can be opened or closed, depending on the weather. The stadium has a steep pointed roof and its outside walls are made of reflective glass. These features are important because of the freezing winter temperatures in Minnesota.

U.S. Bank Stadium hosted Super Bowl LII in 2018.

Minnesota fans refuel with Breakfast and Lunch Nachos. This nacho platter includes scrambled eggs along with cheese, jalapeños, and black beans.

WHERE THEY PLAY

NATIONAL FOOTBALL CONFERENCE

East
1 **Dallas Cowboys** AT&T Stadium
2 **New York Giants** MetLife Stadium
3 **Philadelphia Eagles** Lincoln Financial Field
4 **Washington Football Team** FedEx Field

North
5 **Chicago Bears** Soldier Field
6 **Detroit Lions** Ford Field
7 **Green Bay Packers** Lambeau Field
8 **Minnesota Vikings** U.S. Bank Stadium

South
9 **Atlanta Falcons** Mercedes-Benz Stadium
10 **Carolina Panthers** Bank of America Stadium
11 **New Orleans Saints** Mercedes-Benz Superdome
12 **Tampa Bay Buccaneers** Raymond James Stadium

West
13 **Arizona Cardinals** State Farm Stadium
14 **Los Angeles Rams** SoFi Stadium
15 **San Francisco 49ers** Levi's Stadium
16 **Seattle Seahawks** Lumen Field

SIX

Six Vikings numbers have been retired, including the legendary number 10 worn by Fran Tarkenton.

THE UNIFORMS

The Vikings' iconic purple and gold uniforms are some of the most striking in the NFL. The uniforms have changed very little since the 1960s. The Vikings usually wear purple jerseys with white pants at home. For away games, they wear white jerseys with purple pants. Both uniforms have gold accents.

The Vikings played in all purple for the first time in 1964 against the Detroit Lions. They did not wear all purple again for 43 years. The all-purple combo became the Vikings' **alternate uniform**. It is now worn at least once per season.

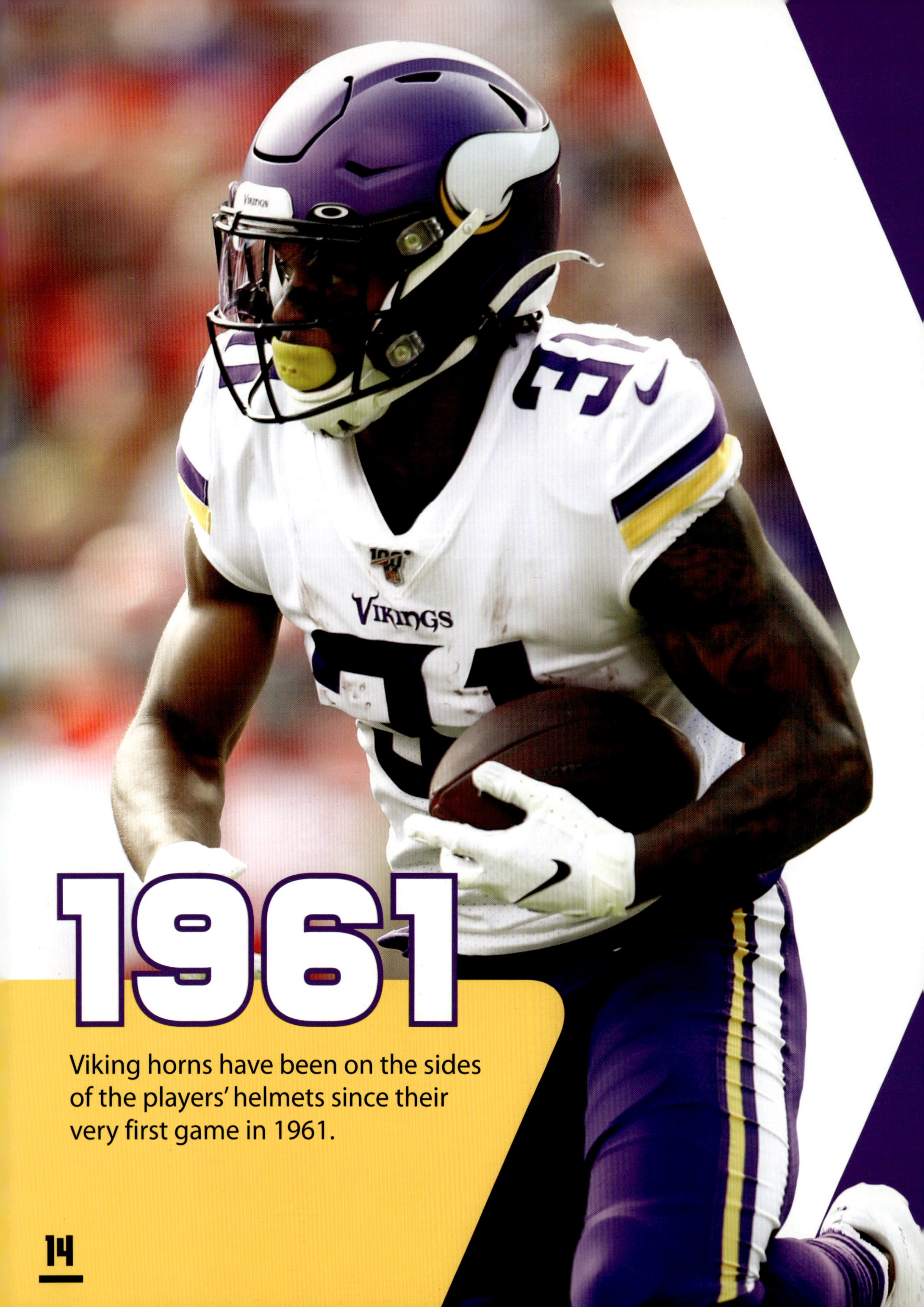

1961

Viking horns have been on the sides of the players' helmets since their very first game in 1961.

THE HELMETS

The Vikings' helmet is instantly recognizable. It is a true **trademark** of the team. The helmets feature a Viking horn on each side. The **logo** honors Minnesota's Viking history. Like the uniforms, the team's helmets have not changed much. The horn design changed slightly in 2006.

A new helmet was released for the 2013 season. Keeping with tradition, it is purple with the white horn "mounted" on gold. Vikings fans are known to wear "Helga" hats to games. They feature white horns and blonde braids.

In 1998, the NFL added a rule requiring all face masks to be transparent.

158

Bud Grant won 158 games as the Vikings' head coach. This was 61 more than Dennis Green, who is number two on the team's win list.

THE COACHES

Owned by lawyer and businessman Zygi Wilf, the Minnesota Vikings are loyal to their head coaches. In 54 years, only nine men have coached the team. Each one has brought a special energy to the Vikings' sideline.

Bud Grant Bud Grant joined Minnesota in 1967. He coached both the offense and defense. Grant was not a fan of indoor practices. He trained his teams outdoors, even during the winter. Grant believed this made his players tougher.

Dennis Green In 1992, Dennis Green became the second African American head coach in NFL history. Under Green, the 1998 season marked a huge breakthrough for the Vikings. Their 15-win season set a team record.

Mike Zimmer Mike Zimmer became the ninth head coach in the history of the Minnesota Vikings on January 15, 2014. Zimmer is known as a tough-minded coach who instills discipline in his players.

Viktor spends his time on the sidelines cheering the Vikings to victory.

THE MASCOT

Viktor carries a hammer. It has a football attached to its golden handle.

Viktor the Viking became the team's mascot in 1960. He dresses as a traditional Viking with long braids and a horned helmet. Viktor supports the Vikings both on and off the field. He visits schools, hospitals, and other places in the Minneapolis community. Viktor enjoys hanging out with young fans in the Vikings' Kids Club. He also sponsors Viktor's Quest to Stop Bullying, a program for local schools.

Viktor wore the traditional fur hat and red coat of the Tower of London guards during a Vikings game in London, England.

LEGENDS OF THE PAST

Many great players have suited up in the Vikings' purple and gold. A few of them have become icons of the team and the city it represents.

Cris Carter

Cris Carter is one of the best pass-catchers the NFL has ever seen. He made eight **Pro Bowls** in his career and was named to the 1990s' NFL All-Decade team. He was voted into the Pro Football **Hall of Fame** in 2013.

Born November 25, 1965, in Troy, Ohio
Position Wide Receiver
16 NFL Seasons (1987–2002)

Jared Allen

Jared Allen began his professional career with the Kansas City Chiefs. He made his first Pro Bowl appearance in 2007 and was then traded to the Vikings. The team made him the highest-paid defender in the NFL. In his first season with his new team, Allen recorded 14.5 **sacks**, while forcing three fumbles.

Born April 3, 1982, in Dallas, Texas
Position Defensive End
12 NFL Seasons (2004–2015)

Fran Tarkenton

Fran Tarkenton was drafted in the third round of the 1961 **NFL Draft** by the Vikings. In his first game, he passed for 250 yards and 4 touchdowns. He also ran for another touchdown. His five touchdowns in an NFL debut is still a football record to this day.

Born February 3, 1940, in Richmond, Virginia
Position Quarterback
18 NFL Seasons (1961–1978)

MODERN STARS

In recent years, the Vikings' team has included many young, talented players. They have proven that they are among the best in the league.

Kirk Cousins

Kirk Cousins was signed by the Vikings in 2018. He was given a huge contract with the hopes he would be their quarterback of the future. In his first season, Cousins showed he could live up to those hopes. He threw for 30 touchdowns and more than 4,000 yards.

Born August 19, 1988, in Barrington, Illinois
Position Quarterback
NFL Seasons 2012–present

Dalvin Cook

Coming out of Florida State, some thought Dalvin Cook might someday be the best running back in the NFL. The Vikings drafted him in the second round of the 2017 NFL Draft. Despite dealing with injuries his first few seasons, Cook has proven to be an explosive runner.

Born August 10, 1995, in Opa-locka, Florida
Position Running Back
NFL Seasons 2017–present

Adam Thielen

Adam Thielen joined the Vikings as an undrafted player in 2013. He played his first regular season game in 2014. During the 2020 season, Thielen had 14 receiving touchdowns.

Born August 22, 1990, in Detroit Lakes, Minnesota
Position Wide Receiver
NFL Seasons 2014–present

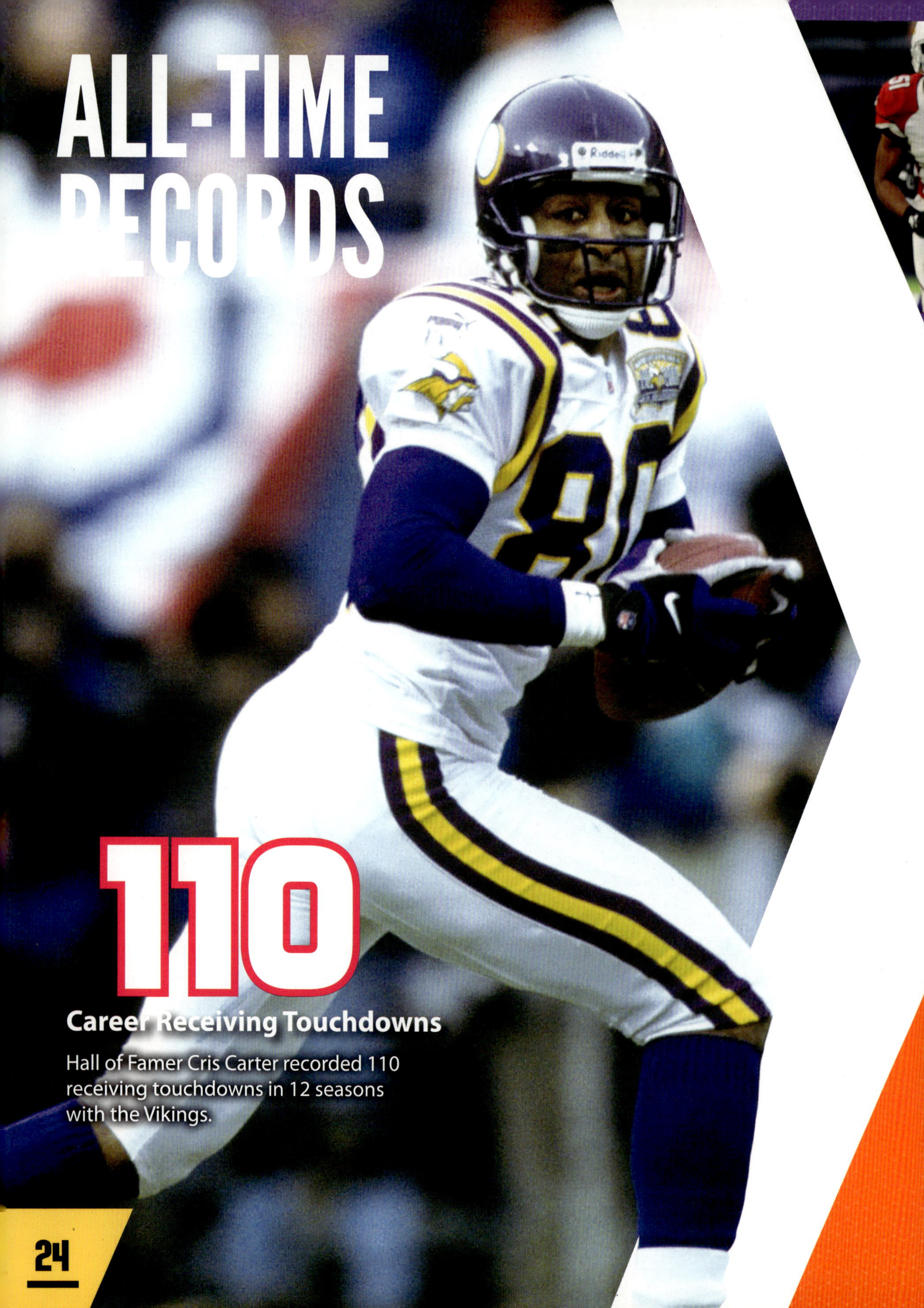

ALL-TIME RECORDS

110

Career Receiving Touchdowns

Hall of Famer Cris Carter recorded 110 receiving touchdowns in 12 seasons with the Vikings.

1,393

Single-Season Kickoff Return Yards

Vikings wide receiver Cordarrelle Patterson grabbed the team record for most kickoff return yards during the 2013 season.

239

Career Passing Touchdowns

Quarterback Fran Tarkenton completed 239 touchdowns while with the Vikings, and 342 in his career.

53

Career Interceptions

Paul Krause's strong defensive play led to eight Pro Bowl appearances in his career. He holds the Vikings' record for career interceptions, with 53.

158

Career Wins

Coach Bud Grant is still the most successful coach in Vikings history, with 158 wins.

1986

Fran Tarkenton becomes the first Viking to be elected into the Pro Football Hall of Fame on August 2, 1986.

VIKINGS TIMELINE

Throughout the team's history, the Minnesota Vikings have had many memorable events. These have become defining moments for the team and its fans.

1960 The Vikings become an official member of the NFL on January 28, 1960.

1970 The Vikings become the first **expansion team** in the NFL to win a championship game.

1998 The team wins their 15th NFC Central Division title, becoming the third team in NFL history to reach the 15–1 mark in a season.

2003 The team's offense ranks first in the NFL for the first time in Vikings history.

2021 The Vikings draft tackle Christian Darrisaw with the 23rd pick of the 2021 NFL Draft.

WRITE A BIOGRAPHY

Life Story

A person's life story can be the subject of a book. This kind of book is called a biography. Reading a biography can help you learn more about a great person.

Get the Facts

Use this book, and research in the library and on the internet, to find out more about your favorite Viking.

Read the questions in the concept web on the following page. Answer the questions in your notebook. Your answers will help you write a biography.

CONCEPT WEB

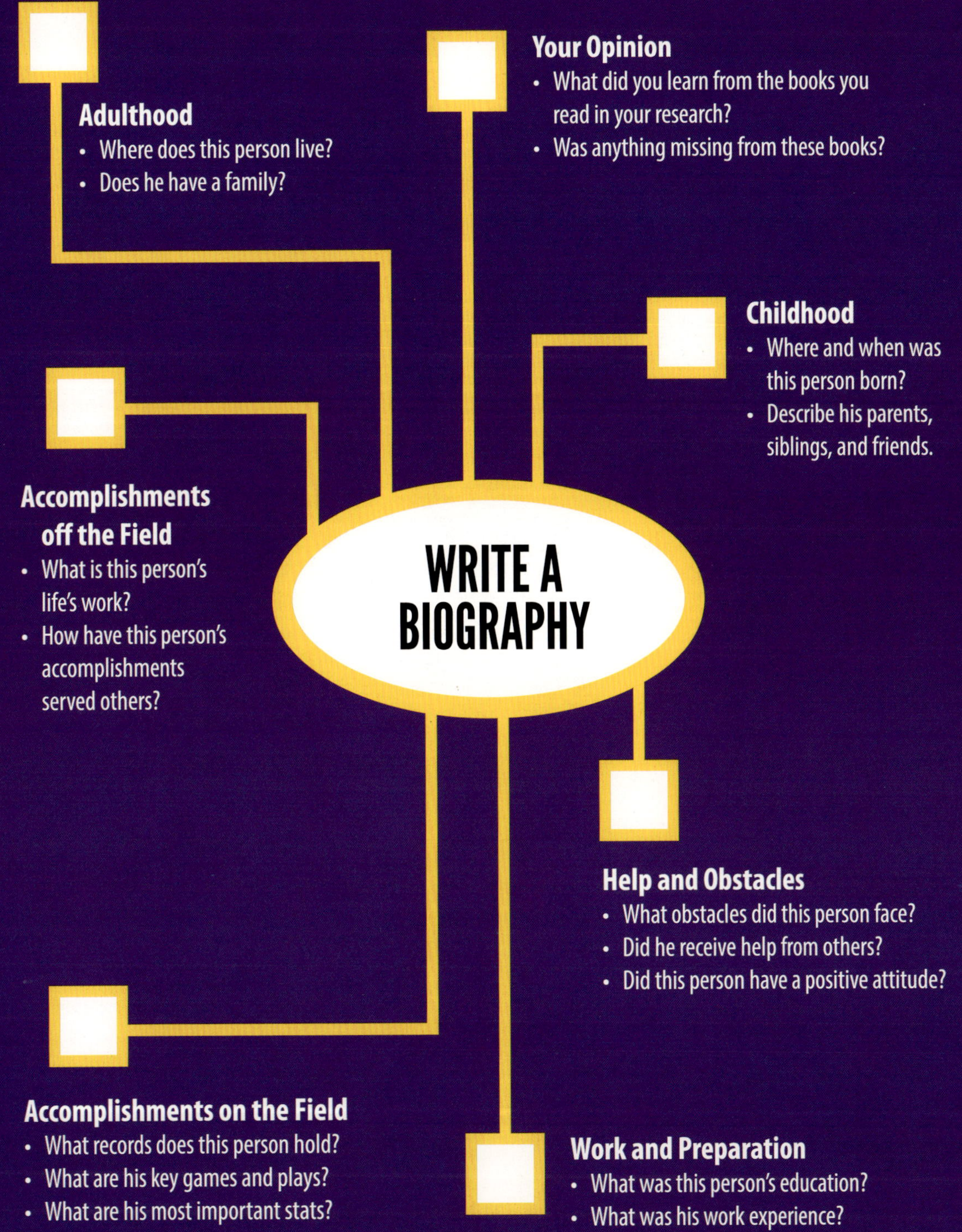

Adulthood
• Where does this person live?
• Does he have a family?
Your Opinion
• What did you learn from the books you read in your research?
• Was anything missing from these books?
Childhood
• Where and when was this person born?
• Describe his parents, siblings, and friends.
Accomplishments off the Field
• What is this person's life's work?
• How have this person's accomplishments served others?
WRITE A BIOGRAPHY
Help and Obstacles
• What obstacles did this person face?
• Did he receive help from others?
• Did this person have a positive attitude?
Accomplishments on the Field
• What records does this person hold?
• What are his key games and plays?
• What are his most important stats?
Work and Preparation
• What was this person's education?
• What was his work experience?

TRIVIA TIME

1 In what year were the Minnesota Vikings formed?

2 Who was the first Viking elected into the Pro Football Hall of Fame?

3 What team record does Cris Carter hold?

4 In which round was Dalvin Cook drafted?

5 What color are the Vikings' home jerseys?

6 What position did Jared Allen play?

7 How many fans can U.S. Bank Stadium hold?

8 What is on each side of the Vikings' helmets?

ANSWERS

1. 1960
2. Fran Tarkenton
3. Career receiving touchdowns
4. Second
5. Purple
6. Defensive end
7. More than 66,000
8. A Viking horn

KEY WORDS

alternate uniform: a uniform that sports teams may wear in games instead of their home or away uniforms

expansion team: a brand-new team in a sports league, usually from a city that has not hosted a team in that league before

hall of fame: a group of persons judged to be outstanding in a sport

logo: a symbol that stands for a team or organization

NFL Draft: an annual event where the NFL chooses college football players to be new team members

playoffs: the games played following the end of the regular season

Pro Bowls: the annual NFL all-star game pitting the best players in the NFC against the best players in the American Football Conference (AFC)

sacks: when quarterbacks are tackled behind the line of scrimmage before they can throw a forward pass

Scandinavian: the people, language, and culture associated with Denmark, Norway, and Sweden

Super Bowl: the NFL's annual championship game between the winning team from the NFC and the winning team from the AFC

trademark: a word or symbol that a person or team is known for

INDEX

Get the best of both worlds.

AV2 bridges the gap between print and digital.

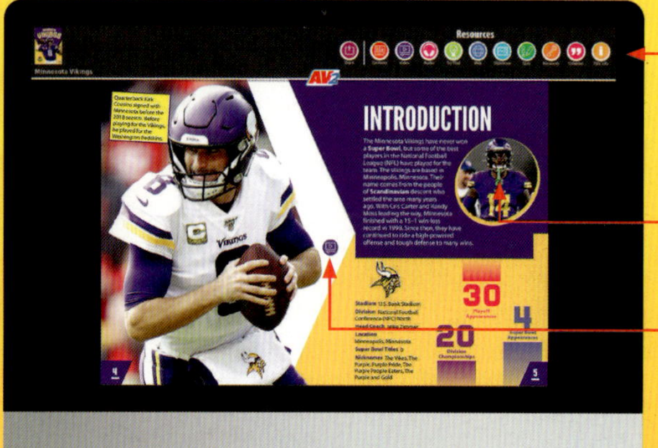

The expandable resources toolbar enables quick access to content including **videos**, **audio**, **activities**, **weblinks**, **slideshows**, **quizzes**, and **key words**.

Animated videos make static images come alive.

Resource icons on each page help readers to further **explore key concepts**.

Published by AV2
276 5th Avenue
Suite 704 #917
New York, NY 10001
Website: www.av2books.com

Library of Congress Control Number: 2020931771

ISBN 978-1-7911-2485-4 (hardcover)
ISBN 978-1-7911-2486-1 (multi-user eBook)

Printed in Guangzhou, China
1 2 3 4 5 6 7 8 9 0 25 24 23 22 21

062021
101320

Art Director: Terry Paulhus Project Coordinator: John Willis

Every reasonable effort has been made to trace ownership and to obtain permission to reprint copyright material. The publisher would be pleased to have any errors or omissions brought to its attention so that they may be corrected in subsequent printings.

The publisher acknowledges Alamy, Getty Images, and Wikimedia as the primary image suppliers for this title.